Fab Girls™ Guide to

Sticky Situations

Edited by Lauren Barnholdt

Discovery Girls, Inc.

CALIFORNIA

Discovery Girls, Inc.
4300 Stevens Creek Blvd., Suite 190
San Jose, California 95129

Fab Girls™ Guide to Sticky Situations
Copyright © 2007 Discovery Girls, Inc.

This book is not intended to replace the opinions or recommendations of the reader's parents, teachers, or other experts or professionals on any of the subjects presented herein. Information, suggestions, and advice in this book are provided solely for the entertainment and as a resource to the reader and are based on research available at the time of publication. The reader should address her individual questions or concerns to her parents, teachers, counselors, physician, and other professionals and experts.

Sticky situation illustrations by Bill Tsukuda.
Book design by Katherine Inouye Lau and Bill Tsukuda.

ISBN 978-1-934766-01-9

Visit Discovery Girls' web site at www.discoverygirls.com.

Printed in the United States of America.

Dedication

Dedicated to the thousands of girls who have taken the time to write to *Discovery Girls* magazine to share your ideas, thoughts, personal stories, and yes, even your problems. All of us who work at Discovery Girls, Inc. have been deeply touched by your letters. You are a constant source of insight and inspiration, and the reason we have created this book.

Acknowledgments

I'd like to send a special thank you to all the girls who have read *Discovery Girls* magazine over the years and have generously shared your thoughts, ideas, and experiences with us. Without you, there would be no *Discovery Girls* magazine and definitely no Discovery Girls books. I feel so very fortunate to have had the opportunity to work with my dedicated and talented staff: Julia Clause, Ashley DeGree, Naomi Kirsten, Katherine Inouye Lau, Alex Saymo, Bill Tsukuda, Sarah Verney, and intern Nick Tran. Your enthusiasm and ability to keep your sense of humor while meeting insane deadlines, your willingness to work long hours, your amazing creative energy, and your insistence on always striving to get better and better have meant more to me than you will ever know—my deepest appreciation! Also, a very special thank you to artists Kathleen Uno, Bill Tsukuda, and Rhiannon Cunag for helping bring the Fab Girls to life. And finally, thanks also to interns Lyn Meheula and Laura Riparbelli. While every book we have published has been very much a group effort, you deserve special recognition for your creative efforts on this book; your writing talents and amazing ideas were truly essential to its creation. Your input has made all of the books so much more fun for girls to read.

Catherine Lee
PUBLISHER
DISCOVERY GIRLS

Meet the Fab Girls

Carmen

Dallas

Hi! We're Carmen and Dallas Fabrulézziano, but you can call us the Fab Girls! Why "Fab"? Well, we came up with that because Fabrulézziano isn't exactly the easiest name to say, and besides, we're totally fabulous! Ha, ha—just kidding.

We may be twins, but we're *totally* different. Carmen plans everything down to the smallest detail—from her glamorous outfits to her perfectly edited homework. She **can't live without her personal organizer**—it even helps her remember the birthdays of practically everyone in the eighth grade! Dallas, on the other hand, is too busy coming up with amazing ideas to organize anything. She's **super smart and super creative,** and you can always count on her to tell you the truth—no matter what! But even though we are so different, **we still make a great team.**

No one ever has a tough time telling us apart, and that's what's so absolutely awesome about being a Fab Girl! Even though **we're complete opposites,** we still share that special sisterly bond that makes us **the best of friends**...well, most of the time!

So, what exactly are we doing here? Discovery Girls asked us to help you through these **crazy, confusing middle-school years.** And who better to go through them with than a couple of fun Fab Girls who know exactly how you feel? We'll give it to you straight and tell you *everything you need to know about sticky situations.* And re-member: With the Fab Girls around, **you're never alone!**

xoxo ♡ Carmen & Dallas

Name: Carmen

Hobbies: Acting, reading romance novels, and perfecting my chocolate-chip cookie recipe.

My biggest dream: To win an Academy Award.

I never leave home without: My planner! It's a minute-by-minute outline of my busy days—dance lessons, friends' birthdays, homework, auditions...I'd be lost without it!

Everyone knows: I'll be totally famous one day! I mean, I already had a small part in a movie...

No one knows: I'm actually very shy. When I have to give a presentation in class, I get totally nauseous.

Biggest pet peeve: People who don't RSVP. I'd love to give half my school a crash course in etiquette!

My take on Dallas: She always knows when I'm feeling down, even if I haven't said a word. She helps me think about things in completely different ways, and I'm my old self in no time!

Name: Dallas

Hobbies: Running track, photography, and playing the drums in my band. (I'm the only girl!)

My biggest dream: Yearbook editor today, world-traveling Pulitzer Prize-winning photojournalist tomorrow!

I never leave home without: Painting a tiny star under my right eye...it's my trademark!

Everyone knows: I'm a math wiz. As math team captain, I totally convinced the principal that we deserve jackets this year.

No one knows: I have a crush on the lead guitarist in my band. (But—SHHH! Don't tell!)

Biggest pet peeve: Girls who gossip and judge others. Don't get me started!

My take on Carmen: She's the most thoughtful sister! Every year on our birthday she creates a new scrapbook for me with highlights of my entire year... with doodles and pictures to match.

Contents

Introduction

Oh, No!

What Do I Do Now?

You're nearly at the bus stop on the first day of school when you suddenly stop dead in your tracks. You've just spotted your BFF. What is that green monstrosity she's wearing? "Don't you just love my outfit?!" she asks, twirling around excitedly. **Your mind races as you try not to panic.** Do you tell her the truth? (As in, "It's the ugliest thing I've ever seen!") Or do you tell her she looks great because...well, won't she be crushed, otherwise? It's a tough one, huh?

Not anymore! Because now you have Discovery Girls' Fab Girls Guide to Sticky Situations—the book that's sure to get you unstuck whenever you find yourself totally glued. **We'll take you through situations from sticky...to stickier...to *stickiest*.** What should you do if you accidentally reveal your best friend's secret crush? Or what if you're the first one in your class to wear a bra—and now you have to change for gym? Or what if you heat up your lunch in the microwave—and it catches fire? Or you overhear a conversation at school that might be about something dangerous about to go down? Never fear! The answers to all these tricky, sticky situations—and many, many more—are all right here!

This is *your* guide. Read it from front to back, or from back to front, or use the table of contents to find the problem you need to solve right now. However you approach it, **you'll soon be an expert on getting unstuck with style.** Being asked out by a boy you don't like? Regret something you said? No sweat for you... because from now on, you'll the best-prepared girl around.

The Editors of *Discovery Girls*

SECTION ONE
Sticky

Chapter One

When Looks Fail

Food in Teeth (and Lots of It)

Sticky Situation #1

You're in the cafeteria having lunch with your BFF when her crush plops his tray down at your table. "Is it okay if I sit here?" he asks, looking a little shy. Score! You *knew* he liked her! You're always telling her that, but she...*uh-oh.* Your BFF flashes a smile, and you realize that she has Oreos all over her teeth! "Sure," she says, still grinning, obviously unaware that she needs a toothbrush STAT. Too bad something about the look on her crush's face makes you think *he* noticed....

You value this friendship? *Help her!* Pull your friend aside and let her know what's up! The easiest way is to say, "I really have to go to the bathroom. Can you come with me for a sec?" Once you're out of sight, she can remove the Oreos. What if your friend won't budge? Maybe she's too into talking with her crush to listen to you. In that case, whisper to her that you need something personal like a tampon or pad. Then, she'll absolutely *have* to come with you...no matter how cute the guy is!

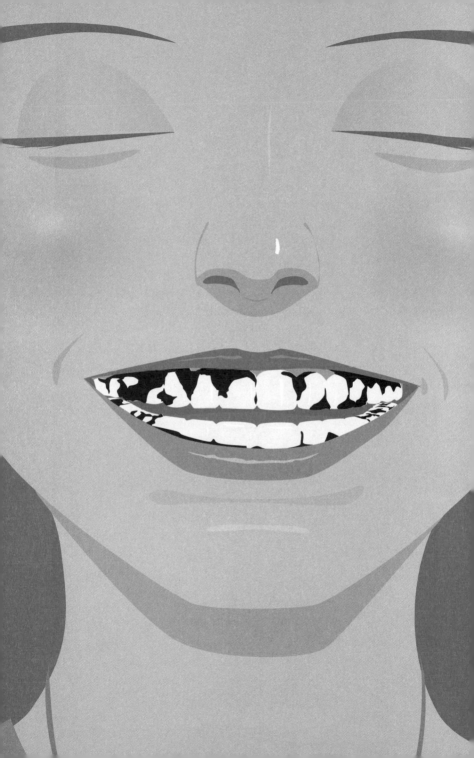

#2 Beyond Bad Hairstyle

To impress your new crush, you went out to get Hannah Montana's pretty blond streaks. Cute, but... the hairstylist thought "Hannah Montana" was the name of a heavy-metal band. Now you're stuck with bright red streaks!

Okay, you have a big choice to make: Keep it or lose it. If you choose to keep it, rock on, sister! You have some amazing, trend-setting confidence! You can work those red streaks like they were meant to be there. If anyone says, "*Eww*, why is your hair like that?!" just proudly respond, "Why isn't *yours?*" People may respect your individuality, and besides, it's awesome to break out from the crowd once in a while. But if you're not feeling that brave, ask your mom to take you back to the salon, or buy a home hair-dye kit to return your hair to its natural color. No time to dye? Just throw on a cute bandanna or hat. That way, all eyes will be on your new accessory, not on your hair.

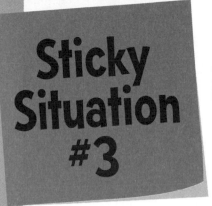

Sticky Situation #3

It's *Not* Pajama Day

Every December 3 since kindergarten has been Pajama Day at your school, and you're totally into it! This year, you don your fave bright pink footie PJs with matching pink slippers, and bring along your teddy bear. But when you show up at school—*surprise!* Everyone's wearing their *uniforms*. Turns out the school canceled Pajama Day—and you're the only one who didn't know.

You have two choices: Either find a way to change ASAP, or embrace the fact that you're dressed for a sleepover. If you decide to change, head to the office and tell them you weren't aware Pajama Day wasn't happening, and ask to call a parent to drop off some regular clothes. If you can't get in touch with your parents, do your best to turn your nightwear into daywear. Throw a sweatshirt over your pajama pants, or borrow something from a friend. If you decide not to change, just tell your classmates that you decided to hold Pajama Day anyway!

Your Sister's Fave Bracelet— Lost!

You borrowed your sister's Italian charm bracelet for your first day of school. (And you totally got compliments on it all day.) But once you get home, the bracelet is gone. It's flown off your wrist like some kind of crazy magic bracelet! Or, maybe, you know, you just...lost it. Okay, don't panic! All you have to do is replace the bracelet before your sis finds out it's gone, right? But then you remember: She bought one of the charms on vacation...in Italy!

First, do a thorough search for the bracelet—at home *and* at school. No good? You have to fess up. Tell your sister how sorry you are, and ask how you can make it up to her. Can you buy her a similar bracelet or do her chores for a week? The consequences of telling the truth may be tough, but the consequences of lying or making up excuses will be tougher! Besides, if you blow this, you may never get access to your sister's amazing closet (and that totally cute pink wrap skirt ...).

Sticky Situation #5

So Not Ready for Picture Day

Your morning beauty routine is a little over-the-top. Shower with your pink loofah, blow-dry your hair, gloss your lips, accessorize....Of course, this takes a little (okay—a *lot*) of time, but it's totally worth it. But this morning your alarm clock didn't go off, and lip gloss was the last thing on your mind as you raced to the bus stop. You were so consumed with getting to school on time that you totally forgot it's picture day. Great! Now your bird's-nest hair and un-washed face will be captured on film for all eternity!

Time to turn your school's bathroom into a beauty salon. Get your friends together, go through their bags, and gather up anything that can help make you photo-ready: barrettes, brushes, hair clips, lip gloss, powder, whatever. Splash some water on your face and tie up your hair in a quick 'do. It's not ideal, but it's better than nothing. Besides, you can console yourself with the fact that there's bound to be a retake day for kids who blink, forget to smile, or, uh, oversleep.

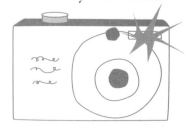

Sticky Situation #6

Chocolate...on Your Pants

Could life get any sweeter? Your latest crush sat at your lunch table, and you've spent the entire period talking. (You have *so* much in common!) When the bell rings, he says, "We should sit together again tomorrow." "Okay," you reply, playing it cool. But when you stand up, you realize you sat on someone's chocolate bar—and now there's a huge brown stain all over the back of your pants. Gross. Your crush looks down and says, "*Eww.* What's that?"

Here's your chance to show your crush you're the kind of girl who can handle anything. Laugh it off, saying, "Oh, yuck—I sat on someone's chocolate bar! Excuse me—I'd better go wash it off." Don't freak out—just keep on playing it cool. You probably won't be able to get the stain out, so if you can, tie a sweatshirt around your waist to hide it. (You don't want to have to keep explaining what happened, because you have better things to do—like thinking about how fab it is to have a new lunch mate!)

BFF in an Awful Outfit

Sticky Situation #7

The first day of junior high is stressful for lots of reasons: new classes, new teachers, new friends. And of course, having to plan the perfect first-day-of-junior-high outfit. You spend hours deciding what to wear, but when you get to the bus stop on the big day, your BFF clearly missed the memo. (You know, the one that said, "Don't wear anything that looks like it's from your grandma's closet.") "Isn't it adorable?" she declares, twirling around in the green monstrosity. "It's vintage!"

You know how you're never supposed to lie? Yeah, well, this is one of those situations that actually demands you *do*. What's worse? Having a little white lie on your conscience, or hurting your BFF's feelings over something as superficial as a dress? Just remember that looks aren't everything, and tell your friend that you admire her creativity and unique style. She definitely won't have to worry about anyone else having her outfit—except maybe a teacher....

Chapter Two

Socially So...Not Cool

Sticky Situation #8

Got a Not-So-Great Gift

Admit it: Your fave part of your birthday is getting presents. Tearing into all those brightly wrapped packages is *fun*, especially when you love what's inside! At your birthday sleepover, you get the best gifts, like a totally cute skirt and some awesome earrings that will go with *everything*. You save the best for last—the present from your BFF. But when you open it, *surprise!* It's a big...animal encyclopedia?! So maybe you *did* mention something once about wanting to be a vet, but, um...hello! "Do you love it?" your BFF squeals.

Okay. Unfortunately, you're about to learn a lesson: It's not about the presents. Look, your BFF gave this to you because she thought you'd love it. In fact, she probably bought it *specifically* with the hope that you would absolutely adore it. Of course, she was *way* off the mark, but still—it came from the heart, so you have to thank her graciously. No need to go over the

top screaming, "*Oooh!* I've always wanted this!" A simple "Thank you so much!" will do fine.

Sticky Situation #9

Embarrassed by Dad

Your basement has everything: a big TV, Ping-Pong, and tons of video games. You love the fact that all your friends love to come over and hang. But then one day your dad decides to ruin all that in the span of, oh, five minutes. He plops down on the couch and starts telling stories about when you were little—including the time you peed your pants in your uncle's living room. Great. Your basement is about to go from hang-out to avoid-out.

Sometimes it seems like there's some kind of rule: If you want to be a parent, you have to turn embarrassing. But try to remember that although *you* see your parent's behavior as embarrassing, your friends probably don't. They might even admire the fact that your dad wants to get to know your friends. Most important, if *you* laugh at your dad, your friends are sure to laugh with you. Come back with something light like, "Yeah, that was hilarious! But not as funny as when *you* had to clean it up!" And then, very gently, tell him it was fun reminiscing with him, but you'll have to catch up with him later. Much later.

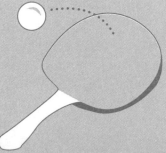

Sticky Situation #10

You're Crushing... He's Not

This is it: You've decided to tell your crush you like him. You're sick of just watching him from across the cafeteria. (You're starting to feel like a bit of a loser, since you have his lunch schedule memorized—pizza on Mondays, bag lunch on Tuesdays...) So after psyching yourself up all week, you walk up to him and say, "I like you." Now he'll say he likes you back, right? But he just gives you a blank stare and says, "Uh..."

Finish quickly with, "You know, as a friend. And a bunch of us are hanging out tomorrow, so I thought you might want to come." You'll cover up your confession, making it sound like your plan all along was to invite him to some group outing. (Note: If there is no group outing, organize one STAT!) Also, keep your cool—don't act any differently around him. Maybe your crush just needs time to get to know you, or maybe he was just shocked when you put him on the spot. Either way, give yourself major kudos for having the guts to put yourself out there.

Dear Diary,

Oh, no! Oh, no...OH, NO! I am SO embarrassed! You know Jeremy, the guy I was
going to ask to the dance, the guy who's
totally adorable and, like, the best player
on the soccer team? Well, I asked him
to the dance today...and the news isn't
good! He said—NO! OMG! I can't believe
that happened! Here's how it went down:
I walked up to him all cutesy and was
like, "Hi, Jeremy, have you heard about
the dance coming up?" He said, "Oh, yeah.
There's actually someone I wanted to ask.
Do you think your sister Dallas would
want to go with me?"

Dallas?! "Um, one moment please," I said,
and then raced into the nearest bathroom.

And here I am now, writing this all
down. I am totally crushed!

 always,
    Carmen

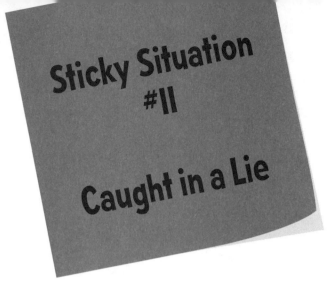

Sticky Situation
#11

Caught in a Lie

Your friend calls you on Saturday afternoon and asks if you want to sleep over. That sounds like fun, but you already made plans to go to a birthday party you know she wasn't invited to. You don't want to hurt her feelings, so you tell her you're sick and even fake a cough for good measure. But the next day *your* mom happens to be talking to *her* mom, and she finds out that you were just fine!

Tell your friend that you *did* want to sleep over but you already had plans. Let her know how much fun you always have at her house, and tell her that you only lied because you didn't want to hurt her feelings. Apologize for making up an excuse, and then, before she can say anything else, ask her if she wants to sleep over at *your* house next weekend. Rent some movies,

make some popcorn, and have an all-night gab session. After a little bonding time, the two of you will be good as new.

Sticky Situation #12

Homework?! What Homework?!

You're sitting in math class, thinking about how boring algebra is and how it figures that you're really good at it, because you'll *never* use it in real life. (Why can't you be good at something that would actually come in handy—like, say, talking to boys?!) And then the teacher says she's about to collect last night's homework. At first you think she's mistaken. There was no homework last night! But as your classmates start rummaging through their binders, you realize *you're* the one who's mistaken...and (*uh-oh*) you have no homework to hand in.

There's really nothing you can do, so try not to freak out. Most likely your teacher already has a policy for late assignments. You might get a zero, or you might just have points taken off if you hand it in the next day. Either way, explain the situation to your teacher, and just be honest. No matter what her policy is, she'll appreciate your maturity in handling the matter. Besides, it's highly unlikely that she'll believe the whole my-dog-ate-my-homework story. (She's totally heard *that* one a thousand times.)

Broke Something Big

While your BFF Emily runs to the bathroom, you start searching through her closet, looking for the perfect outfit for the party you're going to later. All of a sudden you spot what you need: a totally cute baby-blue skirt! You whip it out...and accidentally knock over the lamp on your BFF's desk. It goes crashing to the floor and breaks into a million pieces. To make matters worse, you know the lamp once belonged to her grandmother and is definitely an antique! *Uh-oh!*

You may be tempted to pick up the pieces, shove them into Emily's trash can, and slap an innocent look on your face. ("Broken lamp? What broken lamp?") *Don't.* Really. When you make a mistake like this, it's much better to just come clean. The broken lamp *will* be discovered—and who's going to believe it threw itself off the desk? Tell Emily you understand the lamp probably can't be replaced, but you'd like to try anyway. She'll respect you in the end for being so honest... and you won't have to deal with a guilty conscience.

Dear Diary,

The coolest thing EVER happened today! I was hanging out at my neighbor's house this afternoon. This neighbor, who goes by "Cap'n," has GOT to be 500 years old. Anyway, I let my pet iguana, Hamster, loose when Cap'n went outside to get the mail. Hamster knocked a bottle off of Cap'n's shelf—and it SHATTERED! I was SO scared. What if that was important?!

I decided to tell Cap'n. And he wasn't even mad! He said that it was an old message in a bottle he found on a beach back in his "pirate days." All these years he'd WANTED to read the note, but he'd never had the courage to break the bottle! We read the note together (which was BLANK) and found a little silver coin enclosed (which was cool!)! Cap'n even let me keep it!

So, if you break something, don't keep it quiet!

Later! **Dallas**

Sticky Situation #14

Dark Soda, White Carpet

You and your BFF just rented a cool new movie and you can't wait to watch it. You rush back to your house and hit the kitchen for snacks. (Grape soda, brownies, chips...) But on the way to your room, you trip and spill the soda—all over your mom's white carpet. "Maybe no one will notice," your best friend says hopefully, looking down at the huge purple stain. Yeah, right...

Quick—grab some paper towels and soak up as much of the soda as you can. Then check your mom's cleaning cupboard for a stain remover for carpets. If she has some, read the directions and follow them carefully. If not, look for some seltzer or sparkling water. Pour it onto the stain, then soak it up with clean paper towels. No matter what, tell your mom what happened as

soon as you can. Be sure to add how sorry you are, and that you tried your best to clean it. Then, offer to do something (like extra chores) for the next week to make up for it.

Sticky Situation #15

Stole Something...by Accident

In the locker room after gym, you hear this girl Kelly searching frantically for her tube of cherry pop lip gloss. "Whoever stole my lip gloss is going down!" she yells. You roll your eyes at her over-the-top dramatics. But when you get home that night, you find Kelly's lip gloss in your gym bag. You have no idea how it got there! Fairies? Elves? The real thief, who panicked and dropped it in there?! The point is, it's in *your* bag, and even though it was clearly an accident, something tells you Kelly isn't about to be reasoned with.

If you return the lip gloss, chances are Kelly isn't going to believe you didn't take it. (I mean, come on—would you?) Is there a way you can sneak it back into her bag? If so, go for it. If that's a no-go, consider buying Kelly a new lip balm. Tell her you can't believe someone would take her stuff, and that you bought her another one because you felt so bad. You'll score points for being so nice—and even more if you tell her she should try out for *High School Musical 3*. (Just don't tell her it's because she's such a drama queen....)

Sticky Situation #16

Forgot Lines Onstage

After years of landing nonspeaking roles, you finally snag the role of Annie at your local theater. Yay! You've never been so incredibly happy to be an orphan! Not only that, but a reporter from your local newspaper will be in the audience on opening night! This could totally be your big break. Visions of you starring in the new Olsen twins' movie fill your head. Fab! But on opening night, you walk on stage, the music begins, and…you blank out. The only other "actor" on stage is the dog Sandy, and he's looking at you like, *Come on, Olsen triplet!*

Don't panic. If there's no one backstage ready to whisper your lines to you in an emergency (like this!) you're going to have to just make something up. You know the story and your character, so just go with it. Soon the director will figure out what's going on, someone will step in to save you, and you'll be back on track in no time. (And you can console yourself with the fact that every actress needs to know how to improv, and you just did!)

Sticky Situation #17

Called Someone by the Wrong Name

You tend to get distracted in science because you have a perfect view of your crush, Tyler. One day when Tyler looks particularly cute, your teacher, Miss Stevens, asks you what a sedimentary rock is. You totally know the answer, since you make up for your in-class distraction by studying extra hard *after* school. But when you start to answer, you call Miss Stevens "Tyler"! As in, "Tyler, a sedimentary rock is made up of sediment particles." Everyone laughs, and Tyler turns and looks at you like you've totally lost your mind.

This is super embarrassing, but here's the thing: By fifth period, no one's going to remember this but you. Laugh it off and apologize with something like, "Oh, I'm sorry Miss Stevens. I stayed up late last night and I'm just not thinking this morning." Then turn to your crush and pretend you need to ask him a question, something like, "Yeah, Tyler, I've been meaning to ask you about the homework. Did you understand the third question?"

Chapter
Three

Body Blunders

Sticky Situation #18

Slept in—on a School Day

Every night you remove your favorite silver necklace, slide your hair into a ponytail, and set your alarm. Every single night. In fact, you haven't forgotten to set your alarm once this year, a streak you're totally proud of. But when the power goes out, your fab memory doesn't help. Your alarm clock is flashing two in the morning, but it's actually eight a.m. And your bus comes at 8:05. *Uh-oh.*

It's all about prioritizing. You're not going to have time to watch your favorite cartoon or have homemade pancakes with sliced fruit and whipped cream today. Instead, stick to the essentials—brush your teeth, throw on some (clean!) clothes, grab a granola bar, and get thee to the bus stop! Ideally, you should be planning ahead for days like this (just in case!) by laying out your clothes the night before. Also, tuck a small mirror, hairbrush, and lip gloss into your book bag—then you can use the time on the bus to finish getting ready.

A late start? No prob! I never leave the house without these must-haves in my bag!

Lip gloss. I want my smile to shine, and my lips must be moisturized.

Mini lotion. I don't do dry skin. My skin feels smooth and smells sweet until the last bell rings!

Tissues. For when my allergies flare up—or if my friends and I have some major drama (yeah, I'm talkin' tears)!

Mini toothbrush. You never know when there will be too much garlic in your lunch!

Deodorant. You can keep this in your locker, too. Just have it somewhere!

Pocket mirror. I don't want to run to the girls' bathroom every time I need to check my teeth for stray spinach.

Extra hair things. A hair tie snaps? No prob!

Mini brush. A small way to give your hair big body!

Dallas always says that I'm way high maintenance. But, hey—with my bag by my side, I'm ready for anything!

Sticky Situation #19

Slipped...and Everyone Saw!

Your sister forgot to wake you up (even though you told her three million times your alarm clock was broken), and now you have just one minute to get to the bus stop. You grab your coat, shove your feet into your sneakers, and dash down the icy sidewalk. But just as the bus pulls up, you slip rather spectacularly. Your brand-new shirt rips and your skirt flies up and exposes your undies. Of course, all the kids on the bus come to the windows to gawk. "Are you okay, honey?" the bus driver asks, peering down at you. How embarrassing!

If ever you needed a sense of humor, it's now! So, as long as you're truly not hurt, just stand up and take a bow! Or say something like, "*Oooh*, that was graceful! I guess you won't be seeing me on *Dancing With the Stars*!" And next time, even if you're in a rush, try not to run when it's snowing or icy out. Better to miss the bus than take a chance that you might really get hurt.

Poll: What's the best way to deal with an embarrassing moment?

Laugh at yourself! 60%

Change the subject—pronto! 30%

Turn red...and stay red! 10%

Poll results from DiscoveryGirls.com

Sticky Situation #20

Sneezed During Your Presentation

You've practiced your oral presentation on the Civil War what seems like a billion times—for your mom, your dad, your sister, your stuffed animals, and even your dog. When the big day arrives, you're totally prepared. But then, just as you're about to launch into the reasons for the war, you feel a sneeze coming on. You lift up your hands and—*achooo*! When you move your hands away from your face, there's snot all over them! *Yuck!*

Sneezing in front of the class is not a big deal, as long as you can keep your grace under pressure. Just say "excuse me," and calmly step away to grab a tissue. Wipe off your nose and hands, and then continue with your presentation as if nothing happened. Sneezing is normal, and it's no perfectly okay to stop for a tissue. Chances are, people weren't even close enough to see what happened. By the end of the day, you'll have forgotten it happened—especially when you see you aced your presentation!

Farted in Front of Everyone

Your entire school is crowded into the gym for an assembly. When it's time to start, the principal tells everyone to quiet down. It takes a while (What's up with middle school boys always wanting to be so loud?), but when everyone is finally settled, you accidentally let loose a big stinky one! *Eww.* You hear the girl behind you say, "Someone farted!" as people start turning to look at you...

This can turn into a totally major problem or remain an insignificant mishap—it all depends on *you.* Don't try to blame it on someone else or say something like, "Whoever smelt it, dealt it." That'll draw even *more* attention to you, and besides, people will see right through your defensiveness. The best thing to do is to remain calm, pretend nothing happened, and keep your attention focused on the assembly. Soon everyone will forget about it and turn their attention to something else.

Sweat Stains on *You!*

You're totally proud of the way you played in today's soccer game. You scored two goals and had an awesome defensive play against a girl twice your size. But as you're walking back to the locker room, your good mood is dashed when your friend says, "Hey, you have huge wet marks on your shirt!" You look down to see two dark stains by your armpits. At first, you're confused (How did you spill water all over your jersey?), but then you realize they're sweat marks. That's never, *ever* happened before. You're totally embarrassed, not to mention a little freaked out.

Yeah, we know—at this time in your life, your body seems to be totally against you. But don't worry! It's totally normal, especially when you're pushing your body so hard. Shake it off, and tell your friend that it must mean this was an extra tough game. And before the next one, make sure you wear deodorant and pack an extra stick in your gym bag. Like your grandma always says, an ounce of prevention…

#23 Period on Your Pants

You're sitting in math, totally day-dreaming about Zac Efron (you just know you guys would be a couple if he went to your school), when you get a weird feeling in your stomach. You rush to the girls' room and into a stall...only to discover that you've got your period! And if that's not bad enough, it's starting to leak onto your pants. Yikes!

Stay calm. This is a major bummer, but show us a girl this hasn't happened to and we'll show you...*hmmm*. Well, we'll show you the impossible, since this has happened to *every* girl. If you have a pad or a tampon, use it. (It's a good idea to always have one in your purse or locker.) If you don't, improvise by making a temporary pad from toilet paper or even (really!) a sock. If there's blood on your pants, tie a sweatshirt around your waist or see if any of your friends has a change of clothing you can borrow. Don't be afraid to head down to the nurse for help. Yeah, it might be a little embarrassing, but trust us—she's seen way worse.

Oh, No! No Deo!

It's the morning of your big debate in social studies, and you can't wait to dominate the podium. You're going up against Dylan Smith, this totally obnoxious guy who thinks he's the smartest person in class. But Dylan doesn't know what he's in for—you spent all night memorizing statistics and facts! Bring it on! But as you step off the bus, you realize that you forgot to put on deodorant! *Eww!*

Do you have some deodorant in your locker or gym locker? (If not, consider this a reminder to keep some there from now on.) Out of luck? Improvise. Beg or borrow some perfume or body spray to use on your pits. You can also run to the bathroom during the day and dab your armpits with a wet paper towel and some soap. Try to avoid a lot of physical activity that might make you overly sweaty—this is not the time to showcase your new 50-yard-dash time in gym! And definitely don't let Dylan psych you out and make you sweat, 'cause you're totally going to win the debate.

Dear Diary,

Whew! Everything started off fine this morning, but then...talk about major disaster!

I was doing a big presentation on iguanas in biology and, yes, I was even bringing Hamster with me! I knew my class was going to love him. And I'd done so much research...easy A for me!

As I walked to the classroom, I suddenly felt icky under my arms. Really icky. Wow, I thought. I guess I'm more nervous than I realized! But that wasn't it: I had forgotten to put on deodorant this morning!

Before I completely lost it, I remembered that I'd just washed my P.E. uniform the night before—and it was in my backpack! So I rushed to the bathroom, changed out of my sweaty shirt and into my P.E. tee, and then gave my presentation.

No one seemed to care that I was dressed for running the mile. I guess they were too busy being dazzled by Hamster!

Dallas

Sick at School

You know that nightmare you sometimes have where you're in class and all of a sudden you get a queasy feeling in your stomach? Well, one Tuesday afternoon, that nightmare becomes reality! Before you know it, you're throwing up in the middle of science class. *Eww!* All your classmates turn to look, and some even run outside or plug their noses. Not only don't you feel well, but now you've been completely humiliated in front of your class!

This is *not* the first time someone has barfed in school. Everyone you ask can recall a time when someone threw up in one of their classes—but they probably can't remember who it was, which is good news for you. People *do* understand that you can't help being sick. If anyone gives you a hard time, they're just totally immature. Laugh it off: "Yeah, that was gross! Being sick stinks." In a few days, your nightmare day will be a distant memory.

SECTION TWO
Stickier

Chapter Four

The Friendship Funk

Sticky Situation #26

Friend Spilled Your Secret

You're adopted, but no one in your class knows except your BFF. But then, one day, a kid in your Spanish class pokes you in the side and says, "Hey—what's it like to be adopted? I would *freak out* if my parents weren't really my parents." *How could your friend have told?!*

Yes, your friend *may* have told your secret, but you need to find out exactly what happened. Was it an accident? Did someone else find out and blab? Before marching up to your BFF and calling her a backstabber, give her a chance to explain. If she seems truly sorry, she deserves another chance—after all, everyone makes mistakes (even you!). Next, deal with the issue: Everyone now knows you're adopted. Why is that so terrible? Are you afraid to seem different, or do you think people will make fun of you? If so, take a look around. *Everyone* has something that makes him or her different, and you know your true friends won't care. So embrace it! And now that the secret's out, you can relax. No more worrying about people finding out!

Sticky Situation #27

You Made the Team, Your Friends Didn't

You and your friends have been practicing all week for volleyball team tryouts. On the big day, everything goes according to plan: You ace your serve, and your friends all totally kick butt. Afterward, you're waiting in the gym to find out who made the team. When the coach calls your name, you do one of those totally dorky jump-in-the-air fist pumps. But your good mood is soon deflated. *None* of your friends make the cut!

Eek! This is one of those situations where you feel like you're being torn in two. You're really proud of yourself...but how can you celebrate when your friends look so miserable? The most important thing is to be mindful of your friends' feelings. Congratulate them on their efforts, and remind them that there are other teams they can try out for. Be prepared for them to be a little bit jealous, and wait until you get home before celebrating. You can even tell your parents how humble you were, and make them feel totally obligated to celebrate with you even more!

Sticky Situation #28

First to Wear a Bra

Over the past few months, you've developed at what seems like the speed of sound. No big deal—you've started wearing a bra. (Your mom was actually really cool about it—she took you shopping for bras, which turned into shopping for *clothes*. Yay!) But since none of your friends are developed enough to wear a bra, you've felt weird about mentioning it—and besides, no one seems to have noticed yet. But now you have to change for gym, and that means changing into a sports bra...in the locker room. In front of everyone. *Eek!*

It's hard to be the first one to do anything, and wearing a bra is no exception. You can be proud of your maturity, and just put on your sports bra like it's no big deal. If you don't make a big deal about it, probably no one else will, either. However, if you can't bring yourself to change in front of everyone, just head to one of the bathroom stalls and change in private. Before long, everyone will catch up to you, and no one will give your sports bra a second thought.

Best Friend...
Bad Hairstyle

You know those movies where the shy, quiet girl gets asked to the big dance by the most popular guy in school? And everyone loves the movie, but they're all, "That never happens in real life"? Well, tell them to think again, because it just happened to you! (Okay, it wasn't the most popular guy in school, but he *is* really cute!) On the big night, your best friend comes over to do your hair. "It's going to look just like this," she says, pointing to a pic in a magazine. But once she's finished, it looks more like a nest than a hairstyle.

What would the girl in the movie do? Actually, forget that. This is real life! (And besides, *she* probably got some kind of gorgeous makeover. *Sigh.*) You can't wear a hideous hairstyle to the dance—you'd be completely self-conscious all night! But you *do* have to handle this carefully. Gently steer your BFF in another direction. Say something like, "Wow! It's cute, but I think it would be even cuter if we took out the clips and pulled it up more here." Before long, you'll have fixed the hairstyle—together—without her even realizing you hated it!

Sticky Situation #30

You Didn't Do It!

You're sitting on the couch watching TV when your mom calls you into the kitchen. She says that your friend Molly's mom just called to tell her that you were making up rumors about her daughter...and now Molly's mom wants to talk to you! Shocked, you tell Molly's mom you'd never do that—it must be some sort of mistake! But she won't believe you, and says she doesn't want you hanging out with her daughter anymore.

Okay, so this is totally unfair of Molly's mom and she's just plain wrong. Do not, we repeat, do *not* tell her what you think of her and her lousy accusation. Just *calmly* stick to the facts: You're sorry about what happened, but you didn't do it. You wouldn't do it. End of story. Don't argue, though—if Molly's mom has already made up her mind, you won't convince her. The next day at school, try making your case to Molly. Chances are that if you can convince *Molly* that you didn't make up the rumors, Molly can convince her mom as well.

Sticky Situation #31

You Spilled a Secret

Your BFF announces that she's totally crushing on Danny Jacobs, the cutest boy in the seventh grade. You aren't really that surprised—who *isn't* in love with Danny? She makes you promise not to tell, and of course you agree. You'd never tell a secret. But the next day at school, you're talking to your other BFF and you accidentally let it slip. Oops!

You're not going to like what you have to do. Ready? Tell your friend what happened. We know it's hard, but if she finds out some other way—and she probably will—she'll be even *more* upset. If you're up front and honest, she's less apt to be angry with you. (Plus, you won't have to walk around afraid that she's going to find out.) Be prepared, though—she might be really mad, and it may take her a while to calm down. Just be super nice to her—and yes, maybe even let her borrow that totally cute pink dress of yours that she's always admired. She'll get over it...eventually.

Fab Girls IM Chat

CutieCarmen: Um, Dal?

DaLlAsRoX: Yeah?

CutieCarmen: Well, I've been noticing that u kinda flirt w/ur guitar player & I may have told his friend that u maybe liked him... maybe...oops.

DaLlAsRoX: U WHAT???!!! U better fix this, ASAP!

CutieCarmen: I kno! I'm already thinking up excuses. I could say I was just getting back at u 4 something, or hallucinating...and it's totally NOT true...

DaLlAsRoX: It better work!

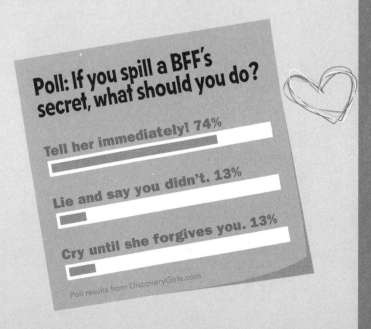

Poll: If you spill a BFF's secret, what should you do?

Tell her immediately! 74%

Lie and say you didn't. 13%

Cry until she forgives you. 13%

Poll results from DiscoveryGirls.com

Blurted Out a Bad Comment

You're having lunch with your friends, and the talk of the table is last night's school talent show. Your friends are going on and on about the skit they performed. (It was some kind of musical number, with a lot of dancing and jumping around.) Honestly, you thought it was kind of dumb, but you would never say that. Until…um…you do, when you accidentally let it slip that you weren't too impressed with their theatrical debut.

Time to backpedal! If the conversation is lighthearted, try throwing in a "Just kidding! Of *course* I thought you guys were fab! In fact, I was totally jealous that I couldn't be in it." Hopefully everyone will laugh it off. If they're not buying it or this kind of remark would seem totally out of place, you're going to have to suck it up and apologize. Hopefully they'll be able to overlook your temporary lapse in judgment. (The same way you overlooked *theirs* when they wore those orange feather dance costumes last night.)

Chapter
Five

Can't We All Just
Get Along?

Sticky Situation #33

Invited to the Party...Late

When you find out your on-again, off-again friend Katie is having a really cool birthday party, you're psyched. On the day she's handing out invitations, you wait for yours to appear in your locker. But at the end of the day, all you see are books and gym sneakers. "Are you going to Katie's party?" another friend asks. You look down at your shoes and admit you weren't invited. Then, two days before the party, Katie comes up to you and practically throws you an invitation. You totally know it was because she *had* to.

Okay, here's the thing: Whether or not she invited you because she "had to," you *have* been invited. (Besides, why not assume the best? Maybe Katie meant to include you all along but forgot to add your name to her list. Or maybe she temporarily misplaced your invitation.) The point is, this is a party you were dying to go to, and now you're invited! Don't create unnecessary drama—just go and have a good time with your friends!

Fab Girls E-mail

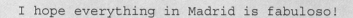

To: Lucia
From: Dallas
Subject: A party problem?

Dear Lucia,

I hope everything in Madrid is fabuloso!

So, I had kind of a crazy week here in the good ol' U.S. of A. On Monday, I found out that Crissy, this really cool girl in my grade, was having a party on Saturday. By Thursday, I hadn't received an invitation. Everyone else in my grade had!

Then this really weird thing happened: The day before the party, Crissy tossed an invitation on my desk and walked away. I'd really (really) wanted to be invited to her party, but not like that! What was up?!

I talked to Carmen about it and she said to just go to the party and have fun. Crissy is one of those really busy girls with a million activities, she said. Maybe she just forgot to give me the invite earlier.

So I did go to the party—and I had a blast! Crissy and I totally bonded during the water-balloon fight (we both have fab aim). And we're planning to hang out—just the two of us—next weekend!

Should I ask her about the invitation thing then? Let me know what you think!

Luv,
Dallas

Sticky Situation #34

Overheard Gossip—About You

You're in the locker room after volleyball practice when you hear a few girls talking on the other side of the lockers. The conversation sounds juicy, and you just can't help but listen in. "She's *so* annoying," one of the girls says. "Totally," someone replies. You bet they're talking about Hannah, this nerdy girl who always moves away from the ball because she's scared of it. But then you realize...they're not talking about Hannah at all—they're talking about *you*!

Okay, this hurts, and there's really no good way to fix it. You can't make people like you, and confronting them might just make it worse. Remember that these girls are *not* your friends, and honestly, you wouldn't *want* them to be. Chances are, if they're gossiping about you, they're also gossiping about each other. So after a breezy, "Bye, girls!" go home and call your BFF. She'll remind you of the awesome, true friends you have by your side, and you'll be able to forget about the gossip posse.

Sticky Situation #35

Invite...or Not?

You finally got your parents to let you have a party at the most fab country club in town. You can't wait to hit the pool and order those yummy sandwiches. But before you can say "fiesta," Mom and Dad decide you can only invite four people. (Totally unfair!) To make things even worse, one of your not-so-close friends sees you passing out invitations. "What's the deal?" she asks, hand on her hip. "How come *I'm* not invited?"

Here's a great rule: *Never* pass out invitations at school. Never! Put in a little extra effort and *mail* them. That way, you avoid this whole scene. Of course, everyone might still find out who was invited—and who wasn't. Nicely explain to those you couldn't invite that your parents would only let you invite a few people. If you're *sure* your parents won't mind, you might add that everyone's coming back to your house afterward to hang, and you hope they'll come. And keep the "My-party's-going-to-be-so-awesome" talk to a minimum. (Of course it is—but you don't have to make the people who weren't invited feel even worse.)

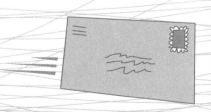

Stuck During Your Friend's Family Fight

You're at your friend Allie's house, leafing through the latest issue of *Discovery Girls* (*love* the swimsuits!), when all of a sudden the door to Allie's room flies open. Her mom bursts in and starts yelling at Allie about a bad grade she received. Yeah, it was a D, but still—this is way over the top! Allie's trying to talk to her mom, her mom's flipping out, and you…well, you're sitting there, wondering what to do.

Can you say "uncomfortable"? *Geez.* Allie's mom should totally have respected the fact that Allie had a friend over and saved the scolding for later. But since Allie and her mom don't seem to realize this, it's time for you to hit the road. Tell them you think it might be better if you came back when things have calmed down. Hopefully they'll realize how inappropriate their behavior is. If they don't, gather up your mags and silently slip out of the room. The last thing this fight needs is someone in the middle of it.

Sticky Situation #37

Surprise Party Oops

You're throwing your BFF a surprise party. After finding the perfect cake recipe and sending out the super secret invitations, everything is set. You're a totally fab party planner—too bad you and your friends can't contain your excitement! You're talking about it at lunch when your BFF walks up, and you all instantly fall silent. "What are you talking about?" she asks. "Nothing," you quickly reply. "Right. Whatever," she says and storms off, thinking everyone was gossiping about *her*.

This is what you get for being a totally awesome friend? *Sigh.* Sure, it's totally unfair, but even though your friend is annoyed now, she will be *so* excited on the day of the surprise. In the meantime, try to make up a little white lie, like, "We were talking about Jenn's crush, and he was right there—that's why we all got quiet all of a sudden." Your BFF should get over it quickly, and you can explain what really happened at her party!

YOU ARE INVITED

Sticky Situation #38

Parents Don't Like Your New Friend

Everyone loves new friends, right? So when you start hanging with the new girl, Roxanne, you know your parents will be psyched. Sure, she's from another school, and no one *really* knows her, but you're sure she's sweet behind all that goth jewelry. But after you invite her over for dinner, your mom pulls you aside and says, "I never want you hanging out with Roxanne again!"

Before you freak out, put yourself in your mom's shoes (even if they *are* totally out of style). She's probably not trying to be mean—she just wants to protect you. Try to figure out why she wouldn't want you hanging with Roxanne. Is she a bit more "mature" than you first thought? Is she always doing things you don't approve of? If not, and your mom is flipping out just because Roxanne lacks table manners or dresses a little, uh, unconventionally, have a talk about it. Explain how important this friendship is to you. (And the next time you have Roxanne over, it may be best to tell her to leave the goth jewelry at home.)

Regret a Comment

There's a new girl at school, and you decide to take her under your wing! Yay for new friends! You spend lunch talking about how you love pizza and old movies, and how you absolutely hate *High School Musical.* The conversation must be a success, because she invites you to sleep over that weekend. But when you get to her bedroom— *surprise!* She has *High School Musical* posters all over her walls.

Yikes! While it may be slightly uncomfortable to realize you dissed her fave movie, she probably doesn't even remember. If she *does* bring it up, say something like, "Yeah, I don't really care for that movie, but your room looks great! I love the colors of your walls!" The most important thing is to let your new bud know that just because you don't like *HSM* doesn't mean that you don't love her!

Fab Girls IM Chat

DaLlasRoX:
Carmen! U there?

CutieCarmen:
Yeah, wats ^?

DaLlasRoX: I let my big mouth run off again!

CutieCarmen: What'd u do this time?

DaLlasRoX: OK, so, u kno Kelsey, right?

CutieCarmen: U mean Kelsey as in "I'm so popular & cute & mean & no1's as good as me"? THAT Kelsey?

DaLlasRoX: That's the 1! ☹

CutieCarmen: Tell me u didn't set that ticking time bomb off!

DaLlasRoX: I definitely did. I accidentally said that she still wets the bed...in front of every1. And she totally found out! She's so after me!

CutieCarmen: U better fix this one ASAP!

DaLlasRoX: I kno! What should I do?!

CutieCarmen: Dal, u have to tell her ur sorry! And make a public announcement that u were totally kidding...then run 4 it!

You've been hearing a new rap song on the radio lately, and it contains a word you've never heard before. It's on the radio, so you figure it's just some harmless slang. But when you start singing the song while riding to a softball game with your friend's family, your friend's father turns around and says, "What did you say? That's a terrible word—it's very racist."

As anyone who has ever been teased knows, words *can* hurt, and racial slurs are as bad as it gets. So even though you didn't mean any harm, you need to apologize. Tell your friend's father that you had no idea the word was offensive, and that you were just singing a song you'd heard on the radio. Then thank him for letting you know it's not something you should be repeating. And remember, there's a lesson here: It's a good idea to find out what a word means *before* you use it!

Sticky Situation #41

Two Tickets, Three People

You and your BFF are *in love* with Miley Cyrus. (You both dressed up as Hannah Montana for Halloween, and you even have matching blond wigs.) When your mom scores two tickets to Hannah's (sold out!) concert, you're psyched. You feel bad that your BFF can't come, but you know your mom is looking forward to some serious mother-daughter bonding. But then your mom says that if you *really* want your BFF to go, she'll stay home. You know your friend would be psyched, but you also don't want to hurt your mom's feelings.

Ask yourself this: How often do you get to hang out with your mom doing something you're *both* excited about? Unless doing the dishes counts, it's probably not that often. If you can tell that your mom really does want to go with you, leave your BFF at home—there are plenty of other ways to have a good time with her *after* the concert. (And be thankful your mom is cool enough to get you tix to Miley Cyrus!)

No Dating Allowed

You're sitting in class when Justin, the boy you've been crushing on forever, walks up to your desk. He looks nervous, which makes *you* nervous. "Hey," he says. "I was just wondering if you'd like to go to a movie with me on Saturday?" *Oh. My. Gosh.* You've been asked on your first date *ever*! Too bad your mom said you can't date until high school...

Tell Justin you have to check with your parents first. Then, talk to your mom. Tell her in a really (really) nice way what's happened. Is there any way she'd be willing to let you go? What if you make it a group date, or if she meets Justin and his parents beforehand? Would she feel better if you invited him to watch a video at your house? If you present all the options in a mature way, you might reach a compromise. But if she doesn't budge, explain to Justin that you tried, but your parents won't let you date until you're older. And don't worry—you *will* get asked out again.

Dear Jason,

I know, I know! Notes are so old-fashioned! Anyway, I just wanted to say that I was so happy when you asked me to go to the movies with you on Saturday night. I've really enjoyed getting to know you better during homeroom and at lunch, so the movie plan sounded perfect! The thing is, my parents won't let Dallas and me date until we're older—much older. So please know that I still want us to hang out and do fun stuff together. I just can't do the "date" thing right now...

Thanks for understanding, J.

Carmen

Poll: Having a boyfriend in middle school is:

Cool, especially if it's my crush! 51%

I'd rather have a boy friend, thanks. 32%

Totally lame! We're too young! 17%

Poll results from DiscoveryGirls.com

Crush Confusion

You're sitting in the cafeteria when Carl Hodge sits down next to you. You've been avoiding him all week, since it's rumored that he likes you, and you're totally not interested. You pretend you don't see him (la la la), but he doesn't budge. "So," he begins, and you know what's coming. "Look," you say. "I know you're going to ask me to the dance, but I don't plan on going." "Oh, uh," he says, looking confused. "I just wanted to know if you could loan me a few bucks for a sandwich." *Oh.*

That's what you get for being Miss Conceited. (Just kidding...sort of.) The only way out of this one is to apologize. Tell Carl you're sorry, and that you shouldn't have assumed he was asking you to the dance. Then loan him some money and send him on his way. And next time, try not to take the words out of people's mouths! They might just surprise you.

Chapter Six

Pressure! Pressure! Pressure!

Mean Teammate

During a soccer game, your teammate, Casey, accidentally kicks the ball out of bounds in the last 30 seconds of the game. Soon after, the team snob, Megan, charges over with her posse and says to Casey, "You know, it's your fault we lost! You totally blew it!" Then Megan turns to you and says, "Don't you agree?"

Don't you just hate mean girls? Standing up to Megan might seem like dooming your social life forever, but remember what they say about karma. If you let Megan get away with putting Casey down, she could turn on *you* next. (And when we say "could" we mean "will." Girls this mean usually end up turning on *everyone* at some point.) So stand up for yourself *and* Casey. Just say, "The loss really lies in *all* of our hands, not just Casey's. I mean, if we'd all played harder, it wouldn't have ended up so close." Chances are, the other girls will agree and back *you* up. And without the support of her posse, Megan will be powerless. (And next time, she'll think twice about pushing you around.)

Party? Parents Say "No"!

Your BFF has convinced her parents to let her throw a boy/girl birthday party. But before you can say "party of the year," your parents totally nix your plans. They don't approve of boys being there! *(Unfair!)* You're miserable, but your BFF is totally unsympathetic. "Best friends come to each other's parties," she says. *"No matter what."*

First, remember that this isn't about your mom versus your BFF. It's about your mom trying to look out for you, and your BFF really wanting you to be there. Talk to your mom. Is there a way to make her feel better about the party? Can your BFF's mom reassure her that the party will be well chaperoned? Can she meet some of the boys beforehand? If she won't budge, don't pitch a fit. Instead, explain to your BFF that you're just as upset as she is. If possible, plan a special day together to make up for it. When your BFF sees that you really do care, she'll get over the fact that you're going to miss her party.

#46 Cyberbullied

You're checking your e-mail while eating your afternoon snack (apples with peanut butter, *mmm*), when you see something that makes you stop mid-bite. A "friend" has sent you an angry e-mail, and she says some pretty nasty things. First you're shocked...and then you're super mad. How dare she! Maybe you should e-mail her back with a piece of your mind!

One problem with the Internet is that it makes it oh-so-easy to fire off a few choice words when you're angry—before you have time to cool down or consider the consequences. Remember, there's a real person on the other end of that e-mail or IM. If you're not willing to say something in person, *don't* put it in an IM or e-mail. Feeling angry? *Step away from the keyboard.* That way, you won't type something you'll regret. (Especially since everything can be printed out for parents to read. Can you type G-R-O-U-N-D-E-D?)

Asked Out, and You Need Out

The rumor mill at school is in full force: Word is you're about to get asked to the spring dance! Too bad the guy who's going to ask you is, um, more dorky than dateable. (His special talent is making fart noises with his armpit.) You try to avoid Armpit Boy, but it's impossible. It's a small school and he's determined. He finally corners you at your locker and pops the question.

Careful! This has to be handled delicately. First, remind yourself that—armpit noises aside—this guy *does* have feelings, and you don't want to hurt them. Besides, you have to give him credit—it takes a lot of guts to ask someone out. So be kind but firm. Say something like, "I'm really flattered, but I can't—I have other plans that night." Or—if you can make this happen—use your girlfriends as an excuse: "I'm really sorry, but my friends and I are all going in a group. Girls only." (And who knows? Maybe Mr. Junior High Armpit Noise Maker will turn into Mr. High School Hottie?! You def don't want to burn *that* bridge!)

Poll: A boy is crushing on you, but you don't feel the same way. You:

Emphasize your friendship in a heart-to-heart. 39%

Ignore him completely. 37%

Have your BFF tell him. 24%

Poll results from DiscoveryGirls.com

Tempted to Cheat

You've enjoyed a string of A's and A+'s in math since, like, kindergarten. You're struggling through this quarter, though, and when it's time for the final test, you know you have to ace it or your average will be ruined. You study and study, but on the day of the test, you're still pretty nervous. Right before it starts, your friend pokes you in the side. "Hey," she says from the seat next to you. "Check it out." And then she opens her binder and shows you a copy of the answer sheet. "You want a copy?"

You most definitely do *not*! Cheating is *never* a good idea. Chances are you'll get caught. Not to mention, you'll feel super guilty afterwards. And are you really going to be happy about your grade if you know you got it by cheating? Your friend won't be angry if you want to take the test on your own, and if she is, she might not be someone you want for a friend anyway. Turn the offer down, and do your best on the test…*without* the answer key.

Poll: If you caught your BFF cheating, what would you do?

Confront her. 71%

Pretend you didn't see. 22%

Cheat along with her! 7%

Poll results from DiscoveryGirls.com

Sticky Situation #49

Pressured by Your Mom

Your school is creating its first-ever field hockey team for girls. *Yawn.* You've never been one for sports, so you don't really pay much attention to the tryout announcements or the flyers in the hall. Your mom, however, has a different opinion. She was the all-star goalie on her high school field hockey team, and when she finds out about the tryouts, she decides you're going to follow in her footsteps. "How fun!" she says, holding up two pairs of cleats. "I didn't know which ones you'd like, so I got both!"

Okay, so the thought of playing field hockey is about as appealing to you as a trip to the dentist. But that's probably just because it's something new and scary. Is there any way you could make field hockey fun? Maybe ask some of your friends to join with you? If you *really* don't want to play, talk to your mom. Make sure you let her know what you'll be doing instead, whether it's writing for the school newspaper or joining the debate team. If you politely explain that *her* dreams are not your dreams, she's sure to understand.

Easy A...or No Way?

After social studies, your teacher pulls you aside and says, "I just wanted to tell you what a great job you did on the Cherokee project! You must have worked so hard, and you definitely deserve the A+ I've given you!" Oh, fab! Except, um, you haven't turned in that project yet—you accidentally left it at home. She must have mistaken another student's A+ project for yours!

You can't take credit for something you didn't do. Sure, it's tempting, but that grade belongs to someone else. Plus, the mix-up will more than likely get sorted out, and then your teacher will ask, "Why did you say this project was yours?" So fess up and tell the truth—your teacher will respect your honesty, and you won't have to walk around on eggshells waiting to be found out.

SECTION THREE
Stickiest

Chapter Seven

Mysterious Messages

Sticky Situation #51

Unknown Screen Name

You're sitting at the computer, putting the finishing touches on an English essay that's due tomorrow (and when we say "finishing touches," we mean, you know, just starting), when an unknown screen name pops up in your IM window. "Who is this?" you type, hoping it's Chase Levy, a boy from your church who's rumored to have a crush on you. But the person starts acting all mysterious, claiming to know you, even though you have no idea who it is.

You should never, *ever* talk to someone online unless you know him or her, since you can easily end up in a dangerous situation without even realizing it. The Internet can be very deceptive—it can seem safe even when it's not. The person behind the screen name may not be who he (or she) is claiming to be—you never *really* know who's on the other side of the computer. Your best bet? Only chat with people you know in "real life." And if you ever receive IM-s from a stranger or e-mails that make you uncomfortable, tell your parents ASAP.

Sticky Situation #52

Mystery Phone Caller

You're home alone on a Sunday night, vegging out with a movie and some popcorn. When the phone rings, you figure it's your BFF, calling for your traditional end-of-the-weekend gab session. "Hello?" you say, settling in for a nice long chat. But it's not your BFF. "Hi, this is your dad's friend from work, Bob." Bob? You've never heard of him. You grab a pad off the table by the phone and get ready to take a message. "Actually," Bob says, "I just need your home address so that I can send your dad some important papers. It would be great if you could just give it to me."

Um, hello?! Is this guy for real? Look, you don't know him. Even if you *have* heard your dad talk about someone named Bob, it's never a good idea to give your address out over the phone. Tell him your dad is busy (*never* say you're home alone) and that if he gives you his number, your dad will call him back soon. If it turns out Bob really *is* who he says he is, both he and your dad will understand. In fact, they'll be proud of you for being so smart.

Sticky Situation #53

Cornered by a Scary Dog

You're walking through the park when this cute dog you've never seen before starts to approach you. *Aw.* You love dogs! "Hey, boy," you say softly, holding out your hand. "Where did you come from?" But then he growls, suddenly looking more killer than cuddly, and starts moving toward you...

Your first instinct may be to turn and run—*don't*. Running will just make the dog want to chase you. Instead, show him that you aren't a threat by keeping your arms at your side and standing still, even if he comes closer to sniff you. Don't make eye contact or smile at him. (He may think you're baring your teeth.) Most likely the dog will lose interest in you and leave. But if he sticks around, wait for signs that he's decided you're okay: His growling has stopped, the fur on the back of his neck is down, and his ears are up. Then *slowly* back away.

#54 Approached by a Stranger

You're shooting hoops in your driveway when a man you don't recognize approaches you and asks if you've seen his lost puppy. "This is him," he says, flashing a pic of a super cute golden retriever. "Can you help me find him? I don't really know the neighborhood, and it will only take a second." You want to help, but you *are* worried about the fact that he's a stranger.

You *should* be worried that this guy is a stranger! Never go off with someone you don't know, no matter what the reason. Tell the guy no, and then head inside. Immediately tell your parents or another trusted adult. This guy may be up to no good, and it's better that you let someone older deal with it.

Sticky Situation #55

Home Alone, Stranger Knocks

You're home alone, working on your dance moves. You're just about to do your signature move (a spin twist into an almost-split), when the doorbell rings. You hear a man yell, "UPS! I've got a package I need you to sign for!" Yay! You've been waiting for some stuff your mom ordered over the Internet. You know you're not supposed to answer the door when you're home alone, but it's the UPS man! What would it hurt, just this once...?

Stop! *Never* answer the door when you're alone. For *anyone*. Even if you think the person on your doorstep is just a delivery man or a neighbor, it's better to play it safe. If it *is* a delivery man, he'll probably leave a slip to be signed and bring the package back the next day. He'll also get back in his truck and be on his merry way in a few minutes. If the person hangs around or tries to convince you to open the door, call your parents or another trusted adult and let them know what's going on.

Sticky Situation #56

A Weapon...at School

You're at your locker, grabbing your stuff for gym class (fitness tests today, *ugh*), when you hear the boy whose locker is next to yours bragging to his friends that he's going to bring a weapon to school tomorrow! You can't tell if he's joking or not, and all the noise in the hall drowns out the rest of the conversation. You head to gym, unsure what to do. He was probably just joking...right?

There is only one thing to do in this situation: *Tell an adult immediately.* Even joking about bringing a weapon to school is not okay—they're dangerous (*duh!*). Maybe the kid is just fooling around, but what if he isn't? If anything happened, you'd never forgive yourself. Tell a teacher now.

Chapter Eight

Stuck!

Sticky Situation #57

Lost in the Woods

It's your first time ever camping at Mt. Shasta. It's so cool—you love the smell of the campfires and the trees, and you can't wait to check the area out. You decide to just go a *little* way into the woods to explore, maybe pick a few wildflowers...but before you know it, you're totally lost.

Don't take a chance that you'll get even farther from the campsite: Find a big tree or a large rock, sit down, and stay put. (Remember, though, you want a resting place, not a hiding place.) If you're with your dog, sibling, or friend, *stay together*. Got a whistle? Three toots indicates distress. Otherwise, sing (it's easier on your vocal chords than yelling) or bang rocks together to help rescuers find you. If you have something white or brightly colored (a bandanna, a piece of paper) make sure it's visible, not tucked away in a pocket. If you're not found by nightfall, cover yourself with leaves to help you stay warm. Most important, don't panic— your parents are probably looking for you already.

Stranded Without a Ride

After a long Saturday at the mall buying clothes and trying out new lip glosses with your BFF, you head to the main doors to wait for the 'rents to pick you up. But when your BFF leaves with her big brother (who just got his license), you're stuck waiting alone. *Bor-ing.* After watching car after car drive by, you're getting antsy. It's been 20 minutes since your friend left, and your ride *still* isn't here. You'd call home, but you don't have a cell phone.

Go back inside the mall and head into a store, restaurant, or kiosk. Ask if you can use the phone. (You can also look for a pay phone, but stay in well-lit areas where there are people around.) If everything is closed, find a security guard to help you. In the future, make a pact with your friend that if you're getting separate rides, you'll wait for each other to get picked up before taking off. (And if you've been begging your parents to get you a cell phone for "emergencies only," now's the perfect time to make your case. We're just saying…)

#59 Forced to Choose Between Divorced Parents

Your parents are getting divorced (ugh) and they still don't know whom you're going to live with (*double ugh*). You're totally bummed—you hate not knowing what's going to happen. And then, just when you think things can't get any worse, your parents say they have to talk to you about the living arrangements. They sit you down and ask *you* to choose!

Choosing between parents is a horrible position to be in. Hello! How can you even *begin* to think about choosing between your mom and your dad? If there's any possible way, try to work out a compromise. Can you switch between the two houses? Live with one parent but visit the other frequently? Take into consideration the practical aspects of one house versus the other. For instance, would you have to switch schools? And is one of your parents better equipped to take care of you? If you *really* can't decide, tell the 'rents that while you're glad they trust you enough to make your own decision, you really need their help on this one.

Sticky Situation #60

Caught Cheating

It's the night before the big Spanish test, and you haven't learned any of your vocab. Figuring it's a lost cause, you go to bed without studying. The next day, as you're taking the test, you discover you can easily see your neighbor's paper...and she always gets A's. You know it's wrong but it's just this once. Before you can turn in the test and make a clean getaway, your teacher notices your wandering eyes, calls you over, and rips up your test!

You made a mistake. It happens. What you did was wrong and no doubt you're going to feel guilty about it. There's really nothing you can do now but apologize to your teacher, tell her you know you made a huge mistake, and spend the rest of the year trying to earn

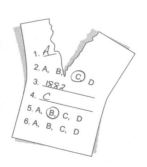

back her respect and trust. How, you ask? By *always* being prepared for class, remembering to study for tests, and being an overall responsible student! If you truly are sorry and don't do it again, you'll be back on track in no time!

Dear Diary,

I am gonna be in SO much trouble! You see, last night I had the option of either studying for my history test or getting the new record that my bandmate Ty just got and LOVES. Musically-obsessed (and stupid) me chose to go record shopping. So this morning at school when our teacher said that the test counts for half of our grade, I freaked. I cannot fail that class!

So, I leaned over in the middle of the test to take a quick peek at my classmate's paper. Before I could even look, I fell out of my chair, and my desk toppled over!

My teacher walked over immediately and ripped my test in half! Now I'll have to do tons of extra credit, AND I have to tell my parents!

Uh-oh...Mom's home. Gotta go.

Dallas

Sticky Situation #61

Hiding a Big Secret

Your dad lost his job a few months ago, and you and the fam had to move from your huge house to a smaller one. You were kind of embarrassed, so you never told your friends what was up. "Hey," your friend says one day when you guys are chillin' at the park. "How come we never hang out at your house anymore?" "Yeah," someone else says. "Why can't we come over?"

Living in a smaller house is nothing to be ashamed of, but it's totally understandable that it's hard to tell your friends your dad lost his job. Unless you're *never* going to have friends over again, at some point you're going to have to come clean about your new digs. How much you reveal, though, is up to you. Maybe you just want to tell your closest friends what happened. Or maybe you don't want to tell anyone. If  your friends ask why you moved, you could just say your parents wanted a smaller house, and leave it at that.

Sticky Situation #62

Pressured by a Friend

You *really* want to spend the night at your friend Karrie's house, but your mom says no because she doesn't know Karrie's parents. So you tell a teeny lie and say you're spending the night at your BFF's instead. But then Karrie starts daring you to do things you *know* are wrong, even dangerous. You just want to go home, but if you call your mom, she'll totally know you lied.

Okay, so now you know that lying to your parents was a really bad idea. Oh well, too late for that now—you're already there. Look, a friend should never pressure you into doing something you don't want to do. Tell Karrie that if she keeps it up, you *will* call your mom. If she doesn't stop, you're going to have to follow through. And, yeah, you might get in trouble, but dealing with the punishment is much better than staying in a weird or dangerous situation. And if you point out to your mom that you did the responsible thing by calling her even though you knew she'd be mad, she might go a little easier on you.

Shoplifting Friend

You're in your fave clothing store with your BFF, trying on shoes and clothes and having a blast. But once you're out of the store with your purchases (new jeans—*yes!*), your friend pulls a necklace out of her pocket. "Hey," you say. "Did you...did you *steal* that?" "*Shhh!*" she says, fastening it around her neck. "Don't worry, it's just a necklace."

Eek! This girl needs a wake-up call before she ends up in deep trouble! Tell her you're not going to hang out with her anymore if she's going to shoplift, and if she ever does it again, you're going to tell your parents. This is going to put a major crimp in your friendship—she's not likely to throw her arms around you and thank you for your concern. But she's totally playing with fire here...and what if she gets caught the next time you're shopping together? You could both end up being charged with stealing. It's so not worth it...no matter how close you two are.

Threatened by the Class Bully

The class bully was making fun of your friend's new braces in math class, calling her things like "braceface" and "metalmouth." (Couldn't he come up with something more original?) "Don't even worry about that jerk," you tell your BFF. But what you don't realize is that the bully is standing right behind you. "I'll be waiting outside for you after school," he growls. *What is with this guy?* you think, and then realize...you're in deep trouble! He's a lot bigger than you, and could probably hurt you if he wanted to. But if you don't show up, everyone will call you a chicken.

Bullies like this are super dangerous—physical violence is not okay. In *any* circumstance. You need to tell a teacher, pronto, before you or someone else gets hurt. And yeah, yeah, you don't want to come off as a chicken or a tattletale, but trust us, anyone who thinks like that isn't worth your time. This is one of those instances where you have to just suck it up and do the right thing—before you or someone else gets hurt.

Sticky Situation #65

Locked Out

After a long day of gossiping in your BFF's backyard, you hop on your bike and head home. But when you get there, your house is locked. Thank goodness you totally know where your key is...too bad it's inside on your dresser, where you left it this morning. No one is home, and you can't go back to your friend's house, because she's already left for dance class!

Ideally, you should make a plan with your parents so you'll know what to do if this happens. (Perhaps you can even hide a key outside.) If it's too late for that, think hard. Is a back window open? Can you get in through the garage? If not, you'll just have to chill until someone comes home. If it's going to be a long time, head to the house of a neighbor you trust and ask if you can call your parents. *Never* go inside your neighbors' house if you don't know them, though— ask them to bring the phone outside to you, or to call for you. And next time, double-check for your key *before* you take off.

Sticky Situation #66

Walked in on Parents... Naked

You just got home from spending the night at your BFF's, where you put that dye in your hair that washes out after three shampoos. You can't wait to freak your parents out with your new look! (Pink hair is totally you!) After checking your hair in the mirror (still pink and still fab, yay!), you run upstairs to show the 'rents. But when you push open the door to their room, they're...omigosh...*naked*!

Your first instinct is probably to yell "Gross! "Disgusting!" and/or "I'm going to barf!" while running screaming down the hall. But resist that impulse—*really*. Just close the door quickly and walk calmly to your room. (And, no—once there, don't IM everyone you know, saying, "OMG, I just walked in on my parents naked!") Your mom or dad might come to talk to you about what happened, or they might decide to pretend it never happened. Either way, they're probably embarrassed, too, so stay calm and let them know you can handle this maturely.

Chapter Nine

Rescue Team!

Sticky Situation #67

Injured Animal

You're walking home from school one day when you hear a weird chirping noise. You look down to see an injured bird lying in the middle of the street! He's so cute, and it looks like he can be saved if you just pull the stick out of his wing. "Hi, little birdie," you say, crouching down. He flutters his wing helplessly. There are cars coming, and you don't want him to get hurt...

While it's tempting to try to help, you should never, ever touch an animal you don't know—especially a wild animal! Birds in particular are known to carry diseases that can infect humans. And although you may think you're helping, you could end up hurting the poor bird even worse. The best way to help him is to hurry home and ask an adult to call your town's animal control center to pick the bird up. You'll stay safe, and the bird will have a better chance of recovery in the hands of professionals.

Runaway Pet

You *love* walking your cute little dog, Monster. (Okay, it doesn't hurt that your crush lives close by, and it totally gives you an excuse to go walking by his house.) One afternoon, as you and Monster are on your fifth trip around the block, he yanks on the leash and goes running down the street. "Monster!" you yell. But he won't stop...and he's running into a busy intersection!

Stop! Chasing Monster will probably just make him run faster, and it might put you in danger. Stay calm and check out the situation. If there's a green light for pedestrians and you can grab Monster (or his leash), do so—carefully. But if the street is way too busy, find an adult who can help. From now on, be a little more cautious, and hold onto that leash. Better yet, the next time you see your crush outside, ask him to walk with you—with two people, it will be easier to keep Monster from taking off.

Sticky Situation #69

House Fire

You're in a totally awesome mood—school is over for the day, you're sitting on your bed reading *Harry Potter and the Deathly Hallows*, enjoying a bowl of ice cream topped with your special homemade hot fudge sauce. (Delish!) But your great mood goes up in flames when you smell smoke coming from the other side of your door!

Uh-oh. Is it possible you forgot to turn off the stove? No matter what, stay calm. If anyone else is home, yell, "Fire!" to alert them to what's going on. Feel your door with the back of your hand. If it's hot, it's best not to open it. Try escaping through a window instead. If this isn't an option and you must go through the door, crawl out, staying low to avoid inhaling the smoke. Once you're out of the house, run to a neighbor's to call 911. And if your clothing ever catches fire, remember: *Stop, drop, and roll!*

#70 Microwave in Flames

You're babysitting the kids next door, and when it's time for lunch, they want hot dogs. So you open the package, wrap a few in aluminum foil, and pop them in the microwave. You're patting yourself on the back for being such a great babysitter...when you realize there's a fire inside the microwave!

First, a word to the wise: *Never* put aluminum foil or any kind of metal in the microwave. Never. (Unfortunately, you just learned this the hard way—*whoops!*) Do *not* open the microwave door. Doing so will only make the fire worse. Instead, leave the door closed—the fire will run out of air and burn itself out. If you can, unplug the microwave, then get yourself and the kids out of the house, and call the fire department from a neighbor's house.

Sticky Situation #71

Tornado Warning

The 'rents are out for the night, and you and your little sis have the house to yourselves. You're sitting around, watching TV, when a special bulletin comes on. At first, you're totally annoyed that they're interrupting your fave show, but your annoyance turns to panic when the announcer says there's a tornado coming. Suddenly, you hear thunder and lightning, and the lights start to flicker...

Don't panic—just do what you need to do to stay safe. If you have an underground cellar or basement, take your little sis down there and wait until the storm passes. If you *don't* have a cellar, stay on the lowest floor of your house. Keep away from windows, and, if possible, take cover in a bathroom or closet, or get under a sturdy table or doorway to protect yourself from falling debris. Stay put until the storm has passed.

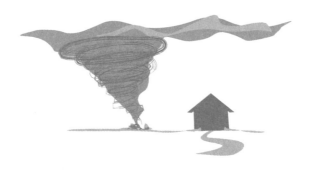

Fab Girls™ Guide to

Friendship Hardship

Friendship help

Meet the Fab Girls

Why Are Friendships So Confusing?

She knows everything about you...she'd never tell your secrets...she's your biggest fan. Who doesn't want a friend like that? **True friendship is a gift...** but it can be hard to find. Whether you're stuck in a fading friendship, caught in the popularity trap, or dealing with mean girls, we'll break down **the solutions** to your problems step by step. Best of all, we'll teach you how to **free yourself from poisonous friendships forever** and be the best friend you can be. Soon, you'll be meeting new people and making friends who truly respect and understand you...because **you deserve first-rate friendships.**

Drama, Drama, Drama

Stuck between friends? Tired of your sibs? Self-conscious about your body? Crushing big time? **You're not alone.** Every month, girls write to Discovery Girls magazine to ask Ali, our **advice** columnist, for **help with issues** like these. When it comes to girls' most troublesome questions, Ali has all the answers you need. Here, she tackles your questions on everything from family to friendship to school to boys...and much, much more. No matter what you're going through, **you'll find answers to your problems inside.** Ali is here to help!

Fab Girls *Guide to*

Getting Through Tough Times

Girls' true stories

Meet the Fab Girls

Getting Over Bad Days

Aubrie's best friend told her they couldn't be friends anymore because Aubrie was "too weird" to be seen with. Torrie was so upset when her parents divorced, she gained 20 pounds and let her grades go into freefall. Mackenzie watched her mom grow sicker and sicker and then die, just when Mackenzie needed her most. **In these amazing true stories,** girls just like you share their private struggles, hoping to help *you* through *your* most difficult times. **You'll find comfort,** encouragement, and inspiration here...and best of all, you'll know that **whatever life throws at you, you are never alone.**